For Elizabeth

Some scenes were first published in *Where's Wally? The Ultimate Fun Book* and *Where's Wally? The Magnificent Poster Book* by Walker Books Ltd, 87 Vauxhall Walk, London SE11 5HJ

This edition published 2009

2 4 6 8 10 9 7 5 3 1

© 1990, 1991, 2009 Martin Handford

The right of Martin Handford to be identified as author/illustrator of this work has been asserted by him in accordance with the Copyright, Designs and Patents Act 1988

This book has been typeset in Wallyfont

Printed in China

British Library Cataloguing in Publication Data: a catalogue record for this book is available from the British Library

ISBN 978-1-4063-2446-4

www.walker.co.uk

WHERE'S WALLY?
THE INCREDIBLE PAPER CHASE

MARTIN HANDFORD

WALKER BOOKS
AND SUBSIDIARIES
LONDON · BOSTON · SYDNEY · AUCKLAND

HI WALLY-WATCHERS!

ARE YOU READY TO JOIN ME ON ANOTHER INCREDIBLE ADVENTURE WITH MORE FUN AND GAMES THAN EVER BEFORE?

I SEE SO MANY WONDERFUL THINGS ON MY TRAVELS THAT THIS TIME I AM TAKING MY NOTEPAD TO HELP ME REMEMBER THEM.

WOW! THE EXCITEMENT BEGINS RIGHT HERE – AS THE RED KNIGHTS STORM THE BLUE KNIGHTS' CASTLE WALLS. CAN YOU SPOT SOME GRINNING GARGOYLES, A GHASTLY GHOUL AND A GIANT CAKE?

THE SEARCH IS ON!

Wally

FIND WALLY, WOOF (BUT ALL YOU CAN SEE IS HIS TAIL), WENDA, WIZARD WHITEBEARD AND ODLAW IN EVERY SCENE. (DON'T BE FOOLED BY ANY CHILDREN THAT ARE DRESSED LIKE WALLY!)

FIND THE PRECIOUS THINGS THEY'VE LOST TOO: WALLY'S KEY, WOOF'S BONE, WENDA'S CAMERA, WIZARD WHITEBEARD'S SCROLL AND ODLAW'S BINOCULARS.

ONE MORE THING! CAN YOU FIND A PIECE OF PAPER THAT WALLY HAS DROPPED FROM HIS NOTEPAD IN EVERY SCENE?

THE JURASSIC GAMES

GOODNESS CRETACEOUS! WHO WILL YOU SUPPORT FROM THE SIDELINES – THE BLUE STRIPY-SAURUS TEAM OR THE PINK SPOTTY-DOCUS TEAM? WILL YOU CHEER FOR THE CRICKET, THE ROWING OR THE BASKETBALL? DON'T FORGET TO WAVE IF YOU SEE A T.REX – THEY'RE NOT IN ANY TEAM, BUT YOU WOULDN'T WANT TO GET ON THEIR WRONG SIDE!

PICTURE THIS

PHEW! LOOK AT ALL THESE FRAMED PORTRAITS. ALTHOUGH THEY MAY BE COLOURED DIFFERENTLY, SOME OF THESE ARE CHARACTERS I HAVE MET ON MY OTHER TRAVELS. THERE ARE ALSO SOME WHO APPEAR ELSEWHERE IN THIS BOOK. CAN YOU SPOT FOUR CHARACTERS THAT APPEAR TWICE IN THIS SPECTACULAR DISPLAY?

WHAT A DOG FIGHT!
BOW WOW WOW! TWO ARMIES ARE LOCKED IN BATTLE, ALL WITH DOG MASKS ON. ONE ARMY IS DRESSED IN BLUE, BLACK AND WHITE, AND THE OTHER IN RED, BROWN AND CREAM. CAN YOU FIND EIGHT SOLDIERS, FOUR FROM EACH SIDE, WITH SOMETHING IN ONE OF THE OTHER SIDE'S COLOURS? OH, AND WHERE IS WOOF IN THIS DOGGY SCRUM?

THE BEAT OF THE DRUMS

BOOM BOOM BADOOM! WHAT AN ORDERLY SCENE! TWO ARMIES ARE STANDING TO ATTENTION SMARTLY DRESSED IN PINK AND BLUE. BUT SOME SOLDIERS ARE LETTING THE SIDE DOWN! CAN YOU FIND THE SOLDIER WHO HAS FORGOTTEN HIS SOCKS AND BOOTS AND 16 SOLDIERS STICKING OUT THEIR TONGUES?

WHERE'S WALLY?
THE INCREDIBLE PAPER CHASE CHECKLIST

THE CASTLE SIEGE

- [ ] Five blue-coated soldiers wearing blue plumes
- [ ] Five red-coated soldiers wearing red plumes
- [ ] A blue-coated soldier wearing a red plume
- [ ] A red-coated soldier wearing a blue plume
- [ ] Four blue-coated archers
- [ ] Five characters holding white feathers
- [ ] Some pike men holding pikes
- [ ] Minors digging a tunnel
- [ ] Twenty-two ladders
- [ ] Some longbowmen wearing long bows
- [ ] Eight catapults
- [ ] Twenty-seven ladies dressed in blue
- [ ] 12 men with white beards
- [ ] A wishing well
- [ ] Two tidy witches
- [ ] Nine blue shields
- [ ] Four horses
- [ ] Three round red shields
- [ ] A prisoner in a puzzling position
- [ ] Eight men snoozing
- [ ] Someone with by far the longest hair
- [ ] A soldier with one bare foot
- [ ] 18 characters with their tongues out
- [ ] Five tents

THE JURASSIC GAMES

- [ ] A dinosaur volleyball game
- [ ] A dinosaur rowing race
- [ ] Dinosaurs playing cricket
- [ ] A dinosaur football match
- [ ] A dinosaur windsurfer race
- [ ] Dinosaurs playing baseball
- [ ] A dinosaur American football game
- [ ] Dinosaurs playing basketball
- [ ] Dinosaurs playing golf
- [ ] A dinosaur steeplechase race
- [ ] A dinosaur polo match
- [ ] Four sets of dinosaur cheerleaders
- [ ] Dinosaurs keeping score with their tails
- [ ] Some showjumping dinosaurs

PICTURE THIS

- [ ] A bird escaped from its frame
- [ ] An angry dragon
- [ ] An aeroplane with real wings
- [ ] An alarm clock
- [ ] A running cactus
- [ ] A cheeky tree trunk
- [ ] Some fish fingers
- [ ] A mermaid in reverse
- [ ] Three skiers
- [ ] A messy eater
- [ ] An upside-down picture
- [ ] A giant foot
- [ ] Three romantic animals
- [ ] A foot being tickled
- [ ] A picture within a picture
- [ ] Two men sharing the same hat
- [ ] Two helmets worn back-to-front
- [ ] Someone drinking through a straw
- [ ] Three flags
- [ ] Nine tongues hanging out
- [ ] A caveman escaped from his frame
- [ ] Seven dogs and a dogfish
- [ ] A bandaged finger
- [ ] A plaited moustache
- [ ] Four bears
- [ ] Three helmets with red plumes
- [ ] Four cats
- [ ] Four ducks
- [ ] Yellow, blue and red picture frames

THE GREAT RETREAT

- [ ] A shield suddenly vacated
- [ ] A heart on a soldier's tunic
- [ ] One curved sword
- [ ] A soldier carrying a hammer
- [ ] One striped spear
- [ ] A soldier not wearing a top
- [ ] Two run-away boots
- [ ] A horseless rider
- [ ] A soldier with a sword and an axe
- [ ] Three bare feet
- [ ] Four pink tails
- [ ] A spear with tips at both ends
- [ ] A helmet with a blue plume
- [ ] A soldier with a red boot and a blue boot
- [ ] A helmet with a red plume

MUDDY SWAMPY JUNGLE GAME

- [ ] An explorer with long sleeves
- [ ] An explorer carrying two spears
- [ ] An explorer wearing a shoe
- [ ] Four contented frogs
- [ ] An explorer with a white beard
- [ ] Five explorers not wearing tops
- [ ] A toe being nipped
- [ ] An explorer wearing a curled-up snake
- [ ] A belt buckled at the back
- [ ] An explorer with two cross-belts
- [ ] Ten butterflies
- [ ] A spear with tips at both ends
- [ ] Eight explorers pointing and laughing
- [ ] Three snapped spears

WHAT A DOG FIGHT

- [ ] A gun dog soldier
- [ ] A guard dog soldier
- [ ] A boxer dog soldier
- [ ] A bloodhound soldier
- [ ] A Great Dane soldier
- [ ] A prize poodle soldier
- [ ] Two soldiers begging for bones
- [ ] Two soldiers running to fetch a ball
- [ ] Four stars on one tunic
- [ ] A dog basket
- [ ] A dog wearing a man mask
- [ ] Two fellow soldiers fighting each other
- [ ] Four ticklish feet
- [ ] A howling dog soldier
- [ ] A soldier with two tails
- [ ] A white star on a cream tunic
- [ ] Cream eyes on a white dog mask
- [ ] A soldier with black and brown legs
- [ ] A soldier with a black arm and a cream arm
- [ ] A cream glove on a blue striped arm
- [ ] A cream glove on a black striped arm
- [ ] A brown dog mask on a blue tunic
- [ ] A blue nose on a brown dog mask

THE BEAT OF THE DRUMS

- [ ] A cheeky back row
- [ ] Courtesy causing a pile-up
- [ ] Some very short spears
- [ ] A group facing in all directions
- [ ] A collision about to happen
- [ ] A knock-on effect
- [ ] Spears held upside down
- [ ] A never-ending spear
- [ ] Two hats joined together
- [ ] Some very scruffy soldiers
- [ ] A soldier wearing only one shoe
- [ ] A soldier wearing red shoes
- [ ] 35 horses
- [ ] A pink hatband and a blue hatband
- [ ] One blue spear
- [ ] One lost shoe
- [ ] One hat with a yellow feather
- [ ] One hat with a red hatband

THE GREAT ESCAPE

- [ ] 10 men wearing green hoods
- [ ] 10 men wearing only one glove
- [ ] 10 men wearing hoods not matching gloves
- [ ] 10 men wearing two different coloured gloves
- [ ] 10 men wearing short and long gloves
- [ ] 10 lost gloves
- [ ] 10 men wearing one fingerless glove
- [ ] Six ladders
- [ ] 19 shovels
- [ ] 5 question mark shapes formed by the hedge

THE ENORMOUS PARTY

- [ ] Five back views of Wally's head
- [ ] A servant bending over backwards
- [ ] Two muscle-men being ignored
- [ ] An eight-man band
- [ ] A punctured tyre
- [ ] A helmet worn back to front
- [ ] Eight front wheels
- [ ] Two upside-down faces of Wally
- [ ] A biker without a motorbike
- [ ] Seven red boots
- [ ] A man wrapped in a streamer
- [ ] A uniform that is too small
- [ ] A uniform that is too big
- [ ] Two men on one motorbike
- [ ] Someone wearing a red tie
- [ ] Someone wearing a blue beret
- [ ] A reluctant arm-rest

THE WACKY WALLY CIRCUS SHOW

- [ ] Four reluctant human canon-balls
- [ ] A clown wearing five hats
- [ ] A clown with a big hooter
- [ ] A bandsman playing bagpipes
- [ ] A bespectacled family of four
- [ ] A bow-tie in a clown's hair
- [ ] An icy iced lolly seller
- [ ] One man supporting three
- [ ] Three straws in one cup
- [ ] Two thirsty clowns
- [ ] A clown used as a broom
- [ ] Three ketchup victims
- [ ] A boy with three drinks
- [ ] A man with six drinks
- [ ] 12 clowns with flowers in their hats

THE ENORMOUS PARTY – ANSWERS

1 France	10 Switzerland	**FLAGS WITH FAULTS**
2 The Netherlands	11 U.S.A.	3 Diagonal red stripes missing
3 United Kingdom	12 Canada	4 Flying the wrong way round
4 Sweden	13 Belgium	5 One star missing
5 Australia	14 New Zealand	11 Red and white stripes reversed
6 Norway	15 Finland	
7 Spain	16 Austria	12 Maple leaf upside-down
8 Japan	17 Federal Republic of Germany	14 Diagonal red stripes missing
9 Denmark	18 Brazil	

PENCIL AND PAPER

Did you find the ten tiny pieces of paper that Wally dropped from his notepad – one in every scene? Wally has left his pencil somewhere on the journey – can you go back and find it super-seekers?

AND TWO MORE THINGS!

Dozens of Wally-watchers appear in this book (there is at least one in every scene but some scenes have many more!).

There's another character – apart from Wally, Woof, Wenda, Wizard Whitebeard and Odlaw – in every scene. Can you find her?

ROLL UP, ROLL UP, ROLL UP
Be happy! Jump for joy!
Dance a dizzy dance!

The Wacky Wally Circus Show
is in town!

THE WACKY WALLY CIRCUS SHOW
THE FOLLOWING PAGES ARE PURELY
FOR YOUR DELIGHT! FOLD OUT THE
PAGES AND PRESS OUT THE ACROBATS,
THE CLOWNS AND THE PUPPETEERS...
TO PUT THE CIRCUS TOGETHER LOOK
INSIDE THE ENVELOPE FOR HELP. NOW
INVITE YOUR FRIENDS, FAMILY AND
PETS TO TAKE THEIR SEATS – THE
MORE THE MERRIER! THEN STRIKE
UP THE BAND! HAND OUT THE
POPCORN AND PUT ON YOUR
VERY OWN SHOW! WOW!